Original title:
The Sea's Reflection

Copyright © 2025 Creative Arts Management OÜ
All rights reserved.

Author: Rafael Sterling
ISBN HARDBACK: 978-1-80587-315-0
ISBN PAPERBACK: 978-1-80587-785-1

Celestial Mirage

In the sky, a fish does glide,
With fins that sparkle, oh what a ride!
A whale wears glasses, peering around,
As dolphins tell jokes, laughter abounds.

A starfish in sandals, struts down the shore,
Holding a drink, asking for more.
Crabs doing cha-chas, shells all aglow,
The tide's just a party, who knew? Let's go!

Nautical Secrets

Octopus in a tux, inked just right,
Serves fishy cocktails under moonlight.
A clam reads a book, 'How to Be Wise',
While eels play charades, much to our surprise.

The parrotfish sings, off-key but proud,
While seagulls gossip, cawing quite loud.
A treasure chest giggles, full to the brim,
With gold that just sparkles, on a whim!

Waves of Wisdom

Seashell secrets are not to miss,
A clam's great advice: 'Give yourself a kiss!'
Turtles in top hats, swimming with grace,
While jellyfish dance, giving quite the chase.

A crab wears a crown, feeling so grand,
With a scepter of seaweed in his hand.
Fish throw confetti, making a splash,
In this watery world, the humor is brash!

Floating Dreams

A buoy plays guitar, strumming at sea,
While mermaids tap toes, full of glee.
Seahorses race, with tails in a twist,
In the floating parade, none can resist.

Barnacles boast of their sticky charm,
As boats pass by, their bells sound the alarm.
A sponge joins the fun, breaks out in song,
In this buoyant world, we all get along!

Where Sky Meets Water

Up high the clouds just dangle,
While fish below start to wrangle.
A seagull jokes, 'I've lost my sock!'
As waves dance on the ocean's clock.

Sunset paints the sky with cheer,
While crabs perform their wiggly leer.
A whale hums tunes, quite jazzed and spry,
While mermaids giggle, passing by.

A Symphony of Salinity

The waves compose a quirky tune,
While jellyfish float like little balloons.
A starfish sings with all its might,
As seaweed twirls in sheer delight.

Conch shells gossip on the shore,
'What's that shell doing? It's such a bore!'
The coral's chuckle makes the tide,
A symphony from deep inside.

Tranquil Beneath the Storm

Raindrops tap like a playful drum,
While fish below wiggle their bum.
Seagulls squawk and take a dive,
As dolphins jump and seem to thrive.

The storm could cause a frightful scene,
Yet waves just giggle, that's their routine.
With surfboards racing, oh what fun!
Under the clouds, they splash and run.

Fathoms of Thought

Beneath the waves, where thoughts collide,
A clam thinks deep, but won't confide.
A turtle grins, a wise old chap,
While sea cucumbers take a nap.

An octopus plays a game of chess,
Casting dilemmas, oh what a mess!
Yet laughter bubbles, rising free,
In fathoms deep, just let it be.

Beneath the Surface

In depths where fish wear silly hats,
And seaweed dances like acrobats,
A crab takes selfies, oh so proud,
While dolphins giggle, laughing loud.

A clam reads poems from a shell,
As jellyfish sway, under their spell,
The anchor's stuck, a ship's great blunder,
As turtles plot their funny wonder.

Currents of Time

A clockfish swims with hands of gold,
Tick-tocking tales that never get old,
Surfers ride waves, but never quite land,
While mermaids craft jokes, perfectly planned.

The tides tease sailors, 'Try to be brave,'
As seagulls squawk, 'You misbehave!'
With sandcastles crumbling under the sun,
"Who needs a crown? We just want fun!"

Reflected Journeys

In a mirror made of shining foam,
Fishes pose for a selfie—oh, how they roam!
Crabs on vacation, sipping warm tea,
As whales tell tales of their last spree.

A lighthouse winks, playing peek-a-boo,
While octopuses paint with colors so blue,
With flip-flops lost at the watery shore,
They say, 'Let's dance; who could ask for more?'

Haunting Echoes of the Shore

Ghost crabs whisper, sharing old fears,
As beach balls bounce, spattering cheers,
The echoes of laughter drift with the tide,
While sandcastles giggle, with nothing to hide.

A pirate's hat sits on a fish's head,
"Join us for tea!" the old shark said,
With flip-flops missing, and shells on the run,
It seems that the beach has just begun!

Cascades of Emotion

Waves crash and giggle, oh what a sound,
Seagulls are cackling, flying around.
A fish wearing goggles, thinks he's so grand,
Dancing with dolphins, in a conga band.

Crabs in tuxedos, with style and flair,
Inviting the clams for a waltz by the pair.
Octopus juggling with a playful grin,
Laughter erupts as the bubbles begin.

Fluid Reveries

A starfish making a fashion mistake,
Wearing a shell like it's all in a shake.
The jellyfish dances, swaying with grace,
But trips on a barnacle—it's now a race!

Seashells are gossiping, tucked in the sand,
Trading their secrets, oh isn't it grand?
An eel slips and slides in a marvelous spree,
Waves of confusion, such a sight to see!

Fragments on the Foam

Bubbles are bouncing, they giggle and pop,
Waves tickle toes on the way to the shop.
A crab with a suitcase, ready to roam,
Almost forgot all the snacks from his home.

Seagulls are squawking, plotting a feast,
They argue over fries, but who gets the least?
Starfish throws parties, invites all the crew,
"Don't forget to RSVP, or I'll be blue!"

Whirlpools of Feeling

A turtle that tripped, on a flip-flop shoe,
Declared it a fashion, that's all he could do.
Fish in a frenzy, with bubbles galore,
They're singing a tune from a Neptune chore.

The waves roll in laughter, tickled and neat,
A crab's on a skateboard, cruising the street.
With a wiggle and giggle, they all join the race,
What a party it is, in this splashy space!

Meditations on the Marsh

There once was a frog with a dream,
To be famous and part of a team.
He practiced his croaks,
Amidst giggles and jokes.

His serenade caused quite a scene,
As ducks quacked in laughs, quite obscene.
They wobbled and spun,
In a dance, oh-so-fun!

A turtle appeared in the mix,
With a hat made of trash and some tricks.
He juggled wet hats,
While avoiding the gnats.

Now the marsh is a stage at high tide,
With critters and creatures all wide-eyed.
They laugh, and they splash,
In a marsh-merry bash!

Songs of the Swell

The waves form a band that won't quit,
With seagulls as vocalists, what a hit!
   They screech while they fly,
      As fish swim on by.

A crab plays the drums in the sand,
With rhythm so catchy, it's grand.
   He snaps with a beat,
      Making beachgoers tap feet.

The starfish, in chords, join the cheer,
Their singing so loud, it draws near.
   With shells in a row,
      They put on a show.

And though they might slip in the sprawl,
They giggle and tumble, having a ball.
   This wild coastal throng,
      Sings a silly, sweet song!

Celestial Waters

Bubbles burst with laughter, bright,
Fish wear top hats, what a sight!
Seagulls gossip, spread the news,
Water dances in vibrant hues.

Crabs clad in jackets, quite the crew,
Playing chess on ocean blue.
Turtles rolling dice for fun,
While the starfish bask in the sun.

Shades of an Endless Expanse

Waves tickle toes, a playful tease,
Sandcastles crumble with the breeze.
Jellyfish wiggle in a shoe,
And dolphins dive to steal your stew.

Seashells chat about the tide,
Urchins giggle, taking pride.
The sun is a clown, wearing a frown,
As waves bounce up to knock him down.

The Silent Symphony

Whales compose a jazzy tune,
With octopuses on bass, oh, such a boon!
Clams snap their shells in rhythm and rhyme,
While the current keeps perfect time.

Seaweed sways like a dancing queen,
As crabs take steps on the marine scene.
The anemones join in with grins,
Swaying like they've had too many spins.

Reflections in a Salted Breeze

Sailboats giggle, tilt and sway,
As gulls get lost in games they play.
Waves whisper secrets, giggling low,
While squids perform a puppet show.

Flip-flops flung in a wild throw,
Chasing fish with a different flow.
A single boot floats by with a pout,
Saying, "I just wanted to stick about!"

Ocean's Embrace

Waves tickle toes on sandy shores,
Seagulls squawk while drenching chores.
Mermaids giggle, swim and play,
Swishing tails in bright ballet.

Turtles dance, they think they're cool,
Flipping flippers, oh, what a fool!
Starfish lounge in their fancy attire,
Dreaming of swimming, like they'd retire.

Portraits on the Surface

A jellyfish wears a floppy hat,
Looking sharp, but oh, so flat.
Crabs compete for the title 'King',
Clacking claws, it's quite a thing!

Dolphins leap with a splashy cheer,
But land in water—oh dear, oh dear!
Octopuses throw an ink-filled bash,
Funny antics in the squishy splash.

Veils of Mist

Fog rolls in like a fluffy cat,
Hiding treasures, where's it at?
Fishermen squint with baited breath,
Hoping for meals, not local myths.

A whale bursts forth in a loud surprise,
Spraying water, oh, what a rise!
Seaweed tickles, it's grown so wild,
Making beachgoers laugh like a child.

Murmurs of the Deep

Fish gossip about the latest trends,
Flipping tails, making silly bends.
Anemones dance to the currents' beat,
While crabs hide, thinking it's neat.

The deep sings songs of silly tales,
Of sunken ships and bubbly gales.
If laughter echoes through ocean skies,
What can be better than fishy hi-fives?

Currents of Change

The fish wear hats and dance with glee,
While jellyfish juggle tea in the sea.
Octopuses play cards; who will win?
With eight arms, cheating's surely a sin!

The tide pulls pranks, it flips the sand,
Seagulls squawk jokes and form a band.
Crabs sidestep gossip, oh what a show,
Even the starfish put on a glow!

Moonlit Mosaics

The moon's a disc, a giant plate,
While clams serve laughs on a silver crate.
Turtles in tuxedos dance in pairs,
Their bow tie knots all tangled in airs.

Dolphins feign naps, sloshing around,
As mermaids snicker, they won't be drowned.
Under the waves, it's quite the blast,
A night full of joy, nothing outclassed!

Journey to the Undercurrent

Bubbles pop loudly, they sing in tune,
A fish with a hat spins under the moon.
Snails race by on a slippery track,
With surfboards made from shells on their back.

Walruses balance on beach balls, oh my!
While sea cucumbers laugh, why even try?
Eels do impressions of synchronized styles,
And everyone giggles in wavy, wild smiles!

Anchored in Blue

The boat wears a hat made of polka dots,
While barnacles gossip, sharing their thoughts.
Waves throw a party; it's quite a blast,
With seaweed confetti, it's a smash hit cast!

Gulls pull pranks, swooping down low,
Dropping their snacks in a silly show.
Fish in bow ties cheer and rejoice,
In this watery world, fun's the best choice!

Reflections in the Mist

In the fog, a fish wore a hat,
Claimed it was stylish, just like a cat.
He danced on the waves, a curious sight,
While seagulls squawked, oh what a fright!

A crab joined the party, pinching away,
Told jokes about clams, oh what a display!
The tide rolled in, with laughter so loud,
As dolphins leaped high, the ocean so proud!

Skyward Waters

A whale in the sky, with wings made of cheese,
Sailed through the clouds, as light as a breeze.
It shouted, 'Catch me, oh fishy friends!'
While turtles below just rolled with the bends!

The octopus spun tales of underwater flight,
Claimed that it moonwalked all through the night.
With each tidal wave, the laughter would swell,
In a world where the weird seemed to fit very well!

Secrets of the Swells

The waves whispered secrets to big sandy toes,
Of mermaids who wore funny hats made of bows.
They giggled and splashed, creating a mess,
As jellyfish joined in, wearing spiffy dress!

A starfish declared, 'I'm the king of the tide!'
But a crab scoffed, 'You're just along for the ride!'
With each ebb and flow, the fun never ended,
In their coastal kingdom, where laughter is blended!

Shores of Silence

On the shores where silence tried to creep,
A clam cracked a joke, and the waves burst to sweep.
The gulls cawed laughter, like a raucous choir,
As seaweed did tango, with gusto and fire!

A turtle in shades, with a surfboard so bright,
Declared, 'I'll catch waves, give it all that I might!'
Yet slipped on a rock, with a sploosh and a grin,
And the whole ocean giggled, 'Let the fun begin!'

Glimpses of One's Soul

I peeked into the water,
Saw my face staring back,
It winked and did a dance,
I laughed till I lost track.

The fish joined in the fun,
They giggled with delight,
Flipping tails in quick sync,
What a splendid sight!

The crab rolled by in style,
Wearing shells like a hat,
He tipped it when he bowed,
And I just sat, chitchat.

The tide pulled in and out,
A game of tag and chase,
I splashed and it splashed back,
We laughed in this wild space.

Harmonies of the Horizon

The sun strums golden rays,
While the seagulls sing off-key,
They chirp the latest gossip,
Of fishy celebrity.

The waves clap like a crowd,
Cheering on the shore's show,
A crab breaks into dance,
And the starfish steals the glow.

With each splash and each glide,
The ocean's voice, so bright,
It cracks jokes with the breeze,
As kites take off with flight.

The clouds float by like balloons,
Dodging the sun's warm beams,
They giggle as they tumble,
In soft cotton candy dreams.

Secret Stories of the Waves

The waves whisper secrets low,
Tales of pirates in disguise,
Of buried treasure long lost,
And mermaids in surprise.

Shells listen closely, nodding,
As barnacles scribble notes,
They plan a swashbuckler ball,
With seaweed as their coats.

Each splash holds a giggle,
A joke from deep below,
Where sea turtles tell tall tales,
Of jellyfish in a show.

The sharks don party hats,
While dolphins flip and twist,
They organize fun antics,
In that salty, frothy mist.

The Color of Dusk

The sky wears shades of candy,
As night begins to creep,
Stars pop like tiny firecrackers,
And dreams dive in the deep.

The moon paints silver laughter,
On every wave that rolls,
A playful tickle of night,
That whispers to our souls.

Crickets chirp in rhythm,
Like a band of little fools,
They tease the cricket's legs,
With their high-spirited rules.

As I watch the colors blend,
A canvas made in jest,
The night smiles with mischief,
In its whimsical fest.

Whispers of Tidal Dreams

Bubbles pop with giggles loud,
A fish in sunglasses swims the crowd.
Seagulls dance with hats so wide,
A crab in shorts takes a joyful ride.

Waves tickle toes, a funny dance,
Seashells whisper secrets of chance.
Ocean's laughter, a playful tune,
While jellyfish waltz with a swoon.

Beneath the Surface's Gaze

A turtle rides a wave with flair,
While fishy friends throw a funny fair.
Octopus plays the banjo, what a sight,
Tangled up in strings, oh what a fright!

Starfish flip like they own the stage,
Seahorses gossip, smart as a sage.
Underwater pranks, a silly spree,
What a riot beneath the sea!

Echoes of Ocean Depths

A whale sings opera, deep and grand,
While shrimp start a conga, oh so planned.
Clams clap their shells, keep up the beat,
In underwater dances, they can't be beat!

The seaweed sways to the jellyfish band,
While dolphins juggle, it's all so grand.
Lobsters wear ties as they shimmy and sway,
Making snazzy moves that brighten the day.

Waves Cradling Secrets

The tide rolls in, bringing laughter near,
As fish tell tales that we all can hear.
A dolphin's flip steals every show,
While barnacles gossip in a row.

Anemones dance, tickling the sand,
While otters juggle clams, oh so planned.
Each wave a chuckle, each splash a cheer,
When the ocean's alive, it's clear we're here!

Underneath the Ripples

There once was a crab with a hat,
Who danced with a leaping acrobat.
He twirled with a fish,
In a bubbly swish,
And both laughed while maintaining their spat.

A dolphin who loved to play pranks,
Stole shells from the grumpy old shanks.
They'd chase him around,
In a splashy rebound,
While the seagulls just watched with their thanks.

A clam in a booth sold some snacks,
While jellyfish played silly hijacks.
They slipped and they slid,
In a joyfully grid,
Oh, the laughter could fill up the cracks.

The tide surfs in, with a grin,
As creatures all join in the din.
With sillies afloat,
On the waves, they gloat,
And the ocean is where we begin.

The Caress of Salt

A seagull named Lou had a dream,
To sneak past a fish on a beam.
With a wink and a flap,
He fell with a zap,
And landed right in their ice cream!

The octopus dressed up to impress,
In a bow tie, he aimed to redress.
But slipped on some goo,
And before long, who?
He was dancing in mom's little dress!

Crabs in a band try to play,
But the clams just refuse and hooray.
They start up a fight,
For shellfish delight,
And the conch shells all shouted "No way!"

The waves laugh and roll with the tease,
As the tide gets ready to freeze.
More splashes abound,
With the laughter around,
In this salty and bouncy-drenched breeze.

Sea of Soliloquies

A starfish once pondered a tale,
Of barnacles stuck on a rail.
He sighed with his arms,
Fighting all the charms,
Of a life far away in a gale.

A whale with a marvelous grin,
Told jokes that would always win.
The fish would all cheer,
While the sharks disappeared,
From the laughter that sparkled within.

A lobster recited a rhyme,
While others just laughed at the time.
He waved with a claw,
With a comical flaw,
And twisted his body with slime.

The tides roll on in with their flair,
As bubbles dance up in the air.
With humor so bright,
In the soft, salty light,
It's a buoyant world, full of care.

Ephemeral Horizons

A turtle who dreamed of a race,
Found kids with a curious face.
He started quite slow,
But with each little flow,
He leapt like he'd won every place!

Dolphins would leap through the air,
With elegance, flair, and a dare.
They'd twirl in a loop,
And make quite a scoop,
As they whipped with a splash and a flair.

A fish tried to wiggle a dance,
But ended up falling in trance.
With fins in the air,
And bubbles to spare,
He flopped right in front of a prance.

The sunset spills colors, oh neat,
As creatures all gather to greet.
With chuckles that swell,
And stories to tell,
The ocean is quite the retreat.

Embrace of the Shore

A crab tried to dance, oh what a sight,
He twisted and turned, in the moon's light.
But alas, his two left claws did betray,
Tipping over like a boat in dismay.

Seagulls squawked, in laughter they peeped,
As the crab rolled back, his pride now weeped.
On sandy stages, they put on a show,
With shells as the tickets, they'd steal the show.

Shadows and Shimmers

A fish wore a hat, it's true, I swear,
Bobbing along, without a care.
A starfish chimed in with a shell-phone call,
"Can you hear me? I'm having a ball!"

The waves lapped softly, in giggles they glee,
As dolphins performed like acrobats free.
With flips and with flops, they splashed all around,
The ocean's a circus, such joy to be found.

Whispers of the Tides

A clam grinned wide, with pearls to trade,
He opened his shell, "Come see my parade!"
But the tide rolled in and his dreams went away,
He flipped back closed, "I'll save it for May!"

A buoy laughed hard, as he swayed with the breeze,
"Life's but a joke, so let's take it with ease."
The ocean chuckled, in bubbles and foam,
As jellyfish waltzed, feeling right at home.

Mirror of the Waves

A wave took a selfie, splashing with flair,
"Look at my curls! Aren't they rare?"
A fish photobombed, with a big toothy grin,
Said, "Forget the sea, let's start a swim-in!"

Crabs in the back, with a conga line dance,
Pinched each other's toes, they took a chance.
As the tide chuckled hard, and the sun set low,
The ocean's full laughter was the perfect show.

Mirage of the Deep

A fish in a suit, what a sight!
He said, 'I'll swim, but where's my flight?'
With bubbles for shoes and a hat atop,
He danced through the waves, then took a flop.

A crab wears spectacles, looking quite grand,
Claiming he's the wisest in all of the sand.
But when asked for advice, he just does a jig,
And promptly declares, 'I'm too shy, oh big!'

Luminous Horizons

A starfish got lost on a family trip,
It thought it could drive, but forgot how to flip.
It ordered a latte from a clam with a frown,
And ended up planning a beachside renown.

A dolphin in shades buzzes through the tide,
Telling sea-tales of how he can glide.
But trip on a wave, and oh what a splash,
He laughs while he swims, with bubbles to crash.

Chasing the Water's Heart

A turtle in sneakers, fast as can be,
Races a snail who's sipping iced tea.
The crowd of the ocean lets out a cheer,
'You'll win if you hurry, oh dear dear deer!'

A jellyfish juggles, what skill to show,
With lights in the dark, putting on quite the show.
But a fish with a net gets caught in the act,
And floats away laughing, now that's a pact!

Shimmering Veils of Blue

An octopus artist, with eight hands of flair,
Paints a huge mural of seaweed and hair.
But when a seahorse asks for a brush,
It smears ink and bubbles, causing a rush!

A lobster throws parties, with shells for each guest,
Dancing with starfish, who think they're the best.
But when the tide comes and sweeps them away,
They giggle and say, 'Let's do this again, hey!'

Ethereal Palettes

Colors dance on the waves,
Like a party for fish and their graves.
An octopus dons a bright pink hat,
While crabs do the cha-cha with a splat.

The seagulls squawk a tune so bold,
Trading tales of treasures untold.
A starfish poses, striking a pose,
While the fish laugh at whatever's those!

Jellyfish jelly, quite wobbly cheer,
While corals gossip over cold beer.
A dolphin flips, all style and grace,
In a splashy contest, this is their place.

Mermaids giggle with shells in their hair,
Playing tricks on the rest with flair.
A mackerel throws a glittering fist,
In the ocean's ball, who could resist?

The Language of Swells

Waves talk loudly, who knows what they say,
Whispers of crabs as they scuttle away.
A clam's tight-lipped in its sandy lair,
While a fish confides without any care.

Bubble chats give a bubbly shock,
A whale's deep sigh is a tick-tock fox.
Turtles nod like they know the score,
While barnacles argue, 'What's in store?'

Seagulls gossip on the wind's great sigh,
About fishermen who lost their fry.
A ticklish sea urchin shouts, 'That's not fair!'
And a flatfish simply sits, unaware.

Underwater, the concert begins,
With a crab on drums and fish doing spins.
Anemones sway to the uproarious beat,
While a dolphin's dance makes everyone tweet!

Moonbeams on Serene Waters

Moonlight dips like a clumsy ballerina,
Casting sparkles, it's quite the hyena.
A fish winks under the glow so bright,
Says, 'Look at me, I'm the star of the night!'

Crabs play tag with the silvery beams,
While seahorses float on whimsical dreams.
A whale's serenade is the catch of the day,
But it puts all the fish in a grumpy ballet.

Starfish compete for the moon's loving eye,
As jellyfish float, waving their bye-bye.
Mermen have a laugh with a hickory stick,
Playing leapfrog, oh, what a funny trick!

Under the twinkle, they're breeding a story,
Of silly sea pranks and endearing glory.
With bubbles toasting the moonlight's effect,
In this watery world, they dance and collect.

Veils of Tranquility

With each gentle wave, a joke's in the splash,
Barnacles giggle, hoping for cash.
Sea cucumbers pose with a sly little grin,
As they engage in a picnic within.

The sandy floor shuffles, a clam's on the skit,
Dropping its pearl as a crowd wants to split.
'Oh dear!' whispers seaweed, waving with glee,
While tadpoles jiggle in ridiculous spree.

Coral reefs argue who's the best-dressed,
While starfish count shells for a casual test.
Seagulls critique with an eyebrow raised high,
'You call that a color? Oh, please don't lie!'

But underneath it all, peace does abound,
As laughter and whispers ripple around.
In these veils of nature where silliness thrives,
Life's a grand jest, where joy just derives!

Boundless Blue

Waves dance like they mean the show,
Fish wearing sunglasses, going with the flow.
Seagulls squawk hi-five on the beach,
While crabs moonwalk, oh what a reach!

Beach balls soar, with laughs abound,
Sunbathers flip, and sand they mound.
Flip-flops flying, a sprinting feat,
Sandcastles rise, but crumble in heat.

Children chase waves, with squeals that ring,
Sandy dogs join in, doing their thing.
A sunburnt dad basks in glory's light,
While his sandwich flies like a bird in flight.

As tides roll in, humor's at play,
Shells hold secrets, tales of the spray.
Under umbrellas, giggles abound,
The boundless blue always turns around!

Secrets Beneath the Foam

Bubbles giggle as they float away,
A deep-sea fish has something to say.
With a wink and a splash, they trade their tales,
Of underwater parties and sailor fails.

Octopus chefs whip up dinner at eight,
With clam-shell forks and seaweed plate.
Frogfish boast of their latest disguise,
They chuckle at tourists with wide-open eyes.

Starfish stretch, counting seaweed pets,
While turtlenecks wear shells like sun hats, I bet.
Anemones sway, always in vogue,
Planting whispers of their froggy rogue.

In the foam, secrets bubble and burst,
Underwater comedy quenches their thirst.
With a splash and a giggle, the ocean does gleam,
A world ripe with laughter, a hunky-dory dream!

Gaze of the Abyss

Down in the depths, what funny sights,
Creatures in bright colors throw quirky fights.
A fish in glasses reads an old book,
While a whale tells jokes, it's all in the hook.

Anemones dance, twirling in pairs,
Making clumsy moves like they just don't care.
A crab with rhythm leads undersea beats,
While everyone joins, tapping their feets.

Surfaces shimmer, secrets do tease,
With a wink from the clam, laughter's a breeze.
Eels slither through jokes they can't quite share,
Spinning yarns of adventures, with nary a care.

Oh, the abyss holds humor, profound and bright,
Beneath every wave, there's sheer delight.
Fish cracking wise, making life more fun,
In a world where laughter weighs more than the sun!

Lighthouses and Shadows

Lighthouses wink with a bulbous grin,
Casting dreams on waves where jokes begin.
Nautical tales spin wild in the air,
As shadows skip around without a care.

Seagulls in hats direct the fleet,
While dolphins plan a flash mob on the beat.
Crashing waves join in with playful cheer,
Shaking off their salt, spreading good cheer.

Beacons bright lead sailors astray,
With a wink of mischief, come what may.
Tales of lost socks tangled in waves,
Leave sailors chuckling, mere wardrobe braves.

Every flash of light brings giggles to night,
As shadows swirl, dancing with delight.
So here's to the harbor, where laughter runs free,
In lighthouses' embrace, pure joy from the sea!

Blueprint of the Blue

Waves dancing like they're at a ball,
Diving in, I trip and fall.
Seagulls gossip, laughing loud,
Splashing water, I stand proud.

Fish wink, they think I'm keen,
But my flippers? Yes, they squeam.
Mermaids wink, a funny sight,
Sipping tea, oh what a night!

Sunbeams tickle, making way,
Rubber duckies in ballet.
Crabs in suits, they strut and dance,
All around, it's pure romance!

Sandy jokes about the tide,
Throw a shell, hope it won't hide.
Oh, the beach, it's quite the show,
With giggles up and down we go!

Kaleidoscope of Tides

Colors swirl as the waves collide,
Frisbees soar, oh what a ride!
Flip-flop fashion on display,
Suntan lotion gone astray.

Seashells gossip on the shore,
Crabs in hats, they want encore!
Dolphins dance with big grins wide,
Jellyfish twirl with cheerful pride.

Sandcastles rise, a lordly sight,
Tilting towers, wobbly delight.
Palm trees sway, they join the fun,
Underneath the laughing sun!

Ice cream cones in sticky hands,
Trying to make some beachy plans.
Seagulls dive for tasty treats,
While we laugh and wiggle our feet!

Depths of Reflection

Gazing down at the fish parade,
I lost my snack, oh what a trade!
Turtles yawn, they roll their eyes,
Funny things in water-wise.

Mackerels wear a silly frown,
As they try to swim around.
Octopus with eight left feet,
Doing tango, isn't that neat?

Coral reefs in outfits bright,
Hosting parties, what a sight!
Bubble parties, oh what glee,
Who knew fish had such a spree?

Down below, it's all a laugh,
Eels pulling a wiggly craft.
My reflection, a silly view,
Splashing joy, all thanks to you!

Visions at Dusk

Stars peek down, the day's goodbye,
Surfboards whisper, 'Let's fly high!'
Sunset paints the sky with cheer,
On the beach, we've no fear.

Giggling waves with frothy hair,
Crickets chirping, evening flair.
Laughter echoes in the wind,
As dusk brings stories to rescind.

Sand on noses, silly spree,
Glow-in-the-dark fish swim with glee.
Moonbeams join the jokes tonight,
Casting shadows, pure delight.

As we dance with twinkling light,
The seaside magic feels just right.
Waves rush in with playful glee,
In this dusk, we find our spree!

Shores of the Soul

I went to the shore, just me and my hat,
A seagull stole fries and sat on my mat.
The tide came in, oh, what a big splash!
I slipped on some seaweed, fell in with a crash!

My sandals started floating, they look quite divine,
I called out to the fish, 'Come try my wine!'
They giggled and darted, what a flippered crew,
I waved my arms wildly, they waved back too!

A crab offered salsa, I danced on the sand,
He twirled and he swayed, just like a fine band.
The sun was my spotlight, the waves my beat,
We laughed as we grooved, what a jolly treat!

So here by the shore, I've learned life's a jest,
With crabs for my friends, and seagulls as guests.
In waves of laughter, I've found my true goal,
To dance with the tide on the shores of my soul.

Celestial Waters

Stars fell to the ocean, oh what a sight,
I thought I could swim to catch one tonight.
But dolphins came laughing, said, 'What a plan!'
With a flick of their tails, they danced like a band!

I ran in my PJs, took off like a shot,
Got tangled in kelp and forgot what I sought.
But sea turtles chuckled, said, 'You're quite bold!'
As I wrapped in their hugs, my dreams turned to gold.

A starfish called over, said, 'Join in our ball!'
I wobbled and rolled, and I started to fall.
With jellyfish twirling in gaudy attire,
We laughed as they glowed like a new campfire!

So here in the waters, I'm silly and free,
With laughter and bubbles, it's just you and me!
In the waves' silly whispers, I've found my delight,
In cosmic adventures, we dance through the night.

The Dance of Fishes

In the deep, deep blue, there's a fishy parade,
With krill as their dancers, they're not too afraid.
They twirl and they spin, in a watery waltz,
A pufferfish puffed, 'It's not my fault!'

The clownfish told jokes, oh what comic relief,
With bubbles of laughter, they shared their belief.
That underwater parties are all about fun,
And if you can't swim, you just wiggle and run!

They painted my scales with a bright shade of zest,
Said, 'Join our big festa, it's surely the best!'
So I joined in the frolic, got tangled in sea nets,
And we swayed to the rhythm, no signs of regrets!

In this dance of the fishes, my heart found its cheer,
With tales of the ocean, I stayed without fear.
On fins and on laughs, in adventures we bask,
Underwater hilarity, who'd dare to ask?

Dreams in the Current

I floated on dreams, on a giant seashell,
With crabby companions, we all rang the bell.
The waves whispered tales, silly thoughts in a swirl,
As a mermaid swung by, with hair like a twirl!

'Let's catch some moonbeams,' the octopus said,
With eight gentle arms, he spun spaces instead.
We splashed in the moonlight, so bright and so bold,
While the starfish debated what stories are told.

The current was giggling, it tickled my toes,
With dolphins in chorus, singing what nobody knows.
A treasure chest opened, but it held just a shoe,
'Perhaps you're a pirate!' they laughed, 'What to do?'

So here in the current, with laughter galore,
We shared silly moments, like never before.
In dreams that keep flowing, we danced with delight,
In the currents of joy, we're all feeling bright!

Tide's Tender Touch

The ocean waves chuckle and tease,
As they dance on sand with such ease.
A crab in a tux, oh what a sight,
Trying to waltz, it gives me a fright.

Seagulls squawk in a melodious tone,
Stealing my fries like they're their own.
A fish pops up, makes a grand split,
With a flip and a splash, it sure is a hit.

Shells whisper secrets from far-off lands,
While barnacles cling to old, rusty cans.
A beach ball drifts toward a duck's beak,
Only to bounce back with a comical squeak.

And when the tide rolls in for the night,
Even the moon, in giggles, turns bright.
The laughter of waves, what a delight,
As they tickle my toes, all through the night.

The Quiet Between Waves

In the hush between crashes, I hear a sound,
A clam with a joke that's tightly wound.
It cracks up, then shuts its shell with a slam,
As if it just told the world's best jam.

The gulls take a break, they're planning a show,
Strutting around with a flamboyant glow.
They trip on some sand, what a glorious fall,
With ruffled feathers, they giggle, enthralled.

A jellyfish floats by in a nonchalant way,
Seeking attention, it's ready to play.
But eels make a dash with a slick little swirl,
Leaving the jelly in quite a whirl.

The quiet, it swells, like a balloon in flight,
Hiding the chuckles that bubble up bright.
Next wave rolls in with a splash and a grin,
And carries the laughter back out on a spin.

Reflections of Distant Shores

In pools of glass, fish gather to chat,
Debating the finest way to wear a hat.
With bubbles as laughter they pop and they fizz,
Sharing the secrets of how to catch whiz.

A starfish is winking, showing off pride,
As seaweed pirouettes, it takes to the tide.
Crabs juggle shells, their circus is grand,
While the shrimp cheer them on from the sand.

The tides pull back, giving room for play,
As shells sing tunes in a playful array.
With a flip of a tail, a dolphin dives past,
Creating a splash, the laughter holds fast.

Reflections of fun, dancing in spray,
All creatures rejoice at the close of the day.
With flickering light, they mimic the sun,
And share all their laughter, till the day is all done.

Secrets in the Swell

The waves rise up, as curious as cats,
Whispering tales of chipmunk chitchats.
A surfboard drifts near, all haphazard and bold,
While a kid on a floaty refuses to fold.

The tide pulls some toys on a grand escapade,
Bouncing around like a playful charade.
A beach ball escapes and claims it's the king,
To the sandcastles' defeat, it starts its own fling.

The laughter erupts as a seal steals the scene,
Wobbling around like a wobbly machine.
Jellybeans tumble across the fine grain,
Earning giggles from gulls, a delightful strain.

In each lilting wave, there's a secret untold,
Of pranks and of giggles in the salty, the bold.
So join in the fun, let your spirit cavort,
For in this great swell, joy and laughter cavort.

The Liquid Canvas

Waves paint pictures in a jolly way,
Splashing colors on the beach all day.
Seagulls sketch while doing their dance,
Catching fish as if in a trance.

Buckets and spades create silly art,
But jellyfish always play the part.
Kids giggle, making castles of sand,
While crabs march off like a marching band.

Turtles wear hats made from shells they find,
While fish gossip like they're intertwined.
The ocean laughs, with a bubbly cheer,
As waves crash down, it's the funniest sphere!

So let's dip our toes and have a blast,
In this funny world, where time flies fast.
Each moment a splash, each tide a giggle,
On this canvas where we laugh and wiggle.

Secrets of the Surf

The waves whisper secrets, oh so sly,
About fish that wear ties and seagulls that fly.
A shark takes a selfie, with plenty of flair,
While dolphins giggle at the beachside affair.

The sun plays hide and seek with the tide,
While beach balls bounce and kites take pride.
Pelicans perform their dive and soar,
While crabs hold the door, saying 'please, no more!'

Sand castles crumble, but laughter stays strong,
As seaweed wiggles, singing its song.
Watermelons surf in a crazy race,
While children shout, "Hey, that's my space!"

Bubbling treasures under the sun's beam,
Hold funny magic, bursting with dream.
Secrets abound, where we laugh and play,
In the ocean's embrace, come join the fray!

Dancers on the Tide

Waves twirl and swirl, doing a jig,
While starfish twinkle, feeling quite big.
Crabs on the shore groove to a tune,
As fish bust a move under the moon.

The seaweed shakes, in a grasshopper way,
While otters pop in for a fun ballet.
Seagull singers join the shore's reef band,
In hilarious styles, it's perfectly planned.

Flippers flip, and shells cheer along,
As mermaids giggle, harmonizing their song.
The tide keeps the rhythm, a funny beat,
On this dance floor where sea and laughter meet.

Come join the swirl, let your worries slide,
As waves and creatures become your guide.
In the liquid ballroom, silly times abide,
With dancers on the shoreline, our fancies wide!

Beneath the Sky's Embrace

Clouds wear smiles, drifting with ease,
While waves give a wink, tossed by the breeze.
Seashells gather for a gossip spree,
Whispering tales of what's fun at sea.

The sun tells a joke to a sailboat afar,
While jellybeans float, like a candy bar.
Fish on a platter are planning a roast,
And the deep-sea clowns are laughing the most.

Octopuses juggle with questionable grace,
While turtles crack puns, each having their space.
The salty air carries all the delight,
As sunsets remind us of laughter at night.

So gather your dreams, in this light-hearted place,
Where waves and laughter blend with sweet grace.
Under the sky's embrace, you'll surely see,
That fun and joy wash over us like the sea!

Harmony Beneath the Surface

Underwater creatures dance with glee,
A fishy party, come and see!
Crabs wearing hats, oh what a sight,
Dancing with seaweed, feeling just right.

Jellyfish float, like balloons gone rogue,
While clams have a chat, sipping cold grog.
An octopus juggles shells with flair,
Laughing at the waves, without a care.

The starfish debate the best way to lay,
Some think upside-down is the way to play.
Shells clink like glasses, cheers fill the blue,
Under the foam, all silly and new.

Bubbles of laughter rise with the tide,
In this underwater world, we can't hide.
With every splash, joy ignites the scene,
A symphony of silliness, simply serene.

Colors of the Current

The river dances in a rainbow twist,
Fish dress up for a color-filled mist.
A cartwheel eel shows off its bright hue,
While minnows join in, a playful crew.

Green turtles paint murals on the rocks,
While frogs wear shades, keeping time in their clocks.
A crab with a bowtie struts down the lane,
With each ripple giggles spring like rain.

The current giggles, tickling the shore,
Bringing out colors, who could ask for more?
With splashes of orange and splendors so bold,
Nature's canvas, a treasure to behold.

Silly reflections keep game of tag,
In this pool of joy, nothing's a drag.
Every moment a burst of delight,
A carnival of colors, all shining bright.

Shadows on the Shallows

In shallow waters, shadows play hide and seek,
A crab peeks out, feeling quite chic.
The sun winks down, casting silly spots,
Limbo dancing fish are simply hot shots.

Seagulls cackle, their feathers a mess,
Watching the shadows, they can't help but jest.
A stingray performs a graceful flip,
While clams giggle, not wanting to trip.

The swaying kelp is in on the laugh,
Tickling the fins, like a comedic staff.
With playful echoes in every swirl,
The shallow's a stage for each wave and twirl.

A dolphin jumps high, announcing the show,
Its shadow a dancer, stealing the glow.
In this comedy, all feel the vibe,
Where laughter and ripples take the best jibe.

Boundless Reflections

Mirrors of water stretch far and wide,
Where fish brush their scales, taking pride.
A parrotfish poses, with a flash and a grin,
"What do you think? Do I swim with style or sin?"

Seashells gossip, sharing funny tales,
Of sea stars who wore fuzzy detail.
They giggle about crabs in a crazy shoe,
Sprinting on sand, oh what a view!

Eels wrap in knots, playing tug-of-war,
As plucky seahorses dance with galore.
"Try my hairdo," one says with a twist,
In waters reflecting a colorful mist.

With laughter and bubbles floating about,
Every creature shouts, "Let's swim and shout!"
Boundless reflections in playful embrace,
Where nature's a mirror of smile and grace.

Moonlit Ripples

Under a glow of silver light,
Jellyfish waltz, oh what a sight!
They jig and twirl, in bubbles they float,
Dancing like sailors, on a pink goat.

Crabs in tuxedos strut on the shore,
With tiny top hats, they beg for more.
A clam erupts with a laugh so loud,
'What's the catch?' he jokes, feeling proud.

Beach balls roll, the tide waves play,
As seagulls gossip the night away.
In tidal pools, mermaids prepare
With foam and laughter, floating in air.

Upon the sands where tales are spun,
Fish tell jokes, and everyone's fun!
Underneath stars, they share a cheer,
In this watery world, all is clear!

Timeless Currents

Waves slide by with a playful grin,
Sea turtles paddle, where to begin?
One spins about, gets dizzy and lost,
Shouts to a shrimp, 'What's the cost?'

The octopuses play peek-a-boo,
With colors that change like an old shoe.
They tickle the fish, who giggle and glide,
In this underwater humor ride.

Seashells trade secrets, oh what a tale,
One claims it's grand, but slightly stale.
Starfish clap, their applause quite loud,
While the sand gets tickled, feeling proud!

Drifting along in a whimsical sway,
Crabs hold a meeting, then shout hooray!
With laughter and jests, they rule the day,
In currents of joy, they dance and play.

A Dance with the Horizon

A dolphin flips, with great finesse,
'Oh look at me!' is his pretentious guess.
Seagulls squawk as they swoop on by,
Critiquing his form — 'Oh my, oh my!'

The horizon grins, as the sun takes its dip,
With colors on canvas from a comic strip.
Starfish stretch wide, yawning away,
As the tide whispers jokes in a salty play.

A fish in a hat, claims he's quite grand,
Says, 'I'm the king of this land!'
But a crab retorts, in an eloquent way,
'You're dreamin'! Just chill before you sway!'

So under blue skies, they frolic and chime,
Each jest a ripple, a giggle in rhyme.
With breezy delight across the bay,
Life here is a laugh, brightens the day.

Voice of the Waters

Whispers of water, gleefully rise,
Making bubbles with all their prizes.
A turtle chuckles at a passed-out fish,
'Take a sip, it's all that I wish!'

Waves break forth in a comical storm,
As seaweed dances, it bends to the norm.
Clams give a wink, as surfboards go by,
While octopi shout, 'Give it a try!'

Anemones wave, in bright fancy dress,
While crabs on the sand play musical chess.
Each move is a laugh, the tide keeps the beat,
With fins making rhythms, quite light on their feet.

As laughter cascades through oceans so wide,
Every splash brings delight, too hard to hide.
In this merry world, where waters confer,
The voice of the waves brings a jovial blur.

Depths of Solitude

A fish wore a hat, what a sight,
He danced in the waves, feeling bright.
With laughter and bubbles, he swam all day,
Saying, "I'm off to the reef for a play!"

A crab brought a friend, a big octopus,
Said, "Don't mind the mess, it's just our fuss!"
They juggled some pearls, oh what a scene,
While seaweed waved, like a curtain of green.

A turtle once said, with a grin so wide,
"I lost my shell, so now I slide!"
He zipped through the shallows, so slick, so sly,
While fishes all giggled, he passed by.

But then came a wave, through the giggles it roared,
And the fish in the hat? Oh, he soared!
He splashed on a starfish, who just rolled my way,
Yelling, "What a party! Let's surf and play!"

Echoes of the Ocean

A parrotfish squawked, with a wink and a nod,
"I'm the king of this reef, give my fins a prod!"
He threw a small shell, landing right on a snail,
Who frowned and replied, "That's quite rude, you male!"

The jellyfish twirled, with a glittery guide,
Claiming, "I'm the light show! Just watch me glide!"
But tangled in seaweed, she blushed a bright hue,
"Who knew my costume would come off, too?"

A dolphin named Dave, with a flip and a back,
Said, "Catch me if you can! I'm a dolphin, not slack!"
He dove through a wave, but got stuck in the sand,
And giggles erupted, oh wasn't it grand!

Then a crab with a crown said, "Let's vote for our king!"
But no one took him, they were busy to sing!
With sidesplitting laughter, the ocean was bright,
As the fish had a ball, in the shimmering light!

Glistening Horizons

A clam made a selfie, oh what a fuss,
With the sun setting gently, it looked ultra-glamorous.
He smiled with a filter, so pristine, so neat,
While the shrimp in the back danced on their feet.

A whale spouted water, like a fountain of dreams,
Said, "I'm just trying to catch those sunbeams!"
But splashed all the fishes, who tumbled and swayed,
"Next time, dear buddy, maybe just wade?"

A curious eel, dressed up like a king,
Wobbled through kelp, giving everyone bling.
"Look at my scepter! It's made of a shell!"
But it slipped in a current, and he waved, "Oh well!"

With laughter like bubbles, they twinkled, oh true,
Each moment in water was just made for two!
As stars started twinkling, they danced 'til it's late,
In this glistening world where they celebrate fate.

Ripples of Memory

A seahorse recalled, with a glint in his eye,
"We swam with the currents, now look how we fly!"
The turtles all chuckled, joining in the fun,
"Remember the tidal wave, oh what a run!"

The starfish chimed in, with a voice so clear,
"I flipped on the sand, it was my best cheer!"
But when he came back, stuck under the tide,
All the shells rolled, giggling wide.

A pufferfish huffed, he puffed with his might,
"I'm the champion of bubbles, come join my flight!"
His pals laughed and puffed, inflating their laughs,
While tickled by currents, they shared their crafts.

And just when the sun bid a colorful adieu,
A lighthouse winked, sharing all that it knew:
That laughter is treasure, beneath the wide skies,
And every wave carries joy, that never says goodbye!

www.ingramcontent.com/pod-product-compliance
Lightning Source LLC
Chambersburg PA
CBHW060134230426
43661CB00003B/423